Reflections in Modern Waters

Marsha Lenin

BookLeaf Publishing

India | USA | UK

Presentation by *BookLeaf Publishing*

Web: www.bookleafpub.com

E-mail: info@bookleafpub.com

ISBN: 9789358318890

First edition 2023

DEDICATION

To those who marvel at the mundane.

Bleached Corals

It's getting hotter
In my fragile room.

Heat radiates from every crevice,
The warm air moves in elliptical waves,

My surroundings bubble up and evaporate,
Their heavy footprints are callously left behind.

I'm left starving and desperate.
I'm reduced to a brittle shell.

My vibrant skin fades
To a hue akin to melting glue.

Every wave chips away a piece of me,
Fragment after fragment,

Like a poorly plastered wall in a room
Crumbling with every subsequent footstep.

I keep moving.

How else can I escape the impending doom?

Every shudder of the floor
Serves as a reminder of my closeness.

I am almost there.
I see the door through the gathering fog.

I make it to the door.

My fingers contort around the doorknob.

My wrist turns anticlockwise.

As cracks of light slip through the angular shift
of the door,
Everything gives way.

I fall through an invisible hole created for me.
Gravity drags me down multiple levels.

My back faces the ground.
I was unable to turn around

To witness the wonders around me
Blur with increasing intensity.

I could only let nature take its course.

The Seaman's Lament

Illuminate my life,
Dear siren
Erase me from this pitiful existence
Whip me into seafoam.

Let me float on the surface, aerated
With no thought and no purpose.
A cinched blindfold knotted over
My hooded eyelids.

My swelling ears
Pooling with salted water,
Muffled echoes resembling
The whispers imminent
When one listens to a conch shell.

They fail to conceal
Your sultry song that
Leaves me reeling,
Yearning for more,
A compass guiding me to uncharted waters.

You promise to
Lead me to the place where
The algae blooms in its glory.
You assure me to be
Unafraid of the ocean
And the depth that it holds.

You tell me how
Its tides wax and wane with the moon,
How its waves drown and resuscitate.
And yet it stays so blue.
And shines so bejewelled

With the rays of your smile.

Your pearly whites
Suppress my fears.
Your teal tresses
Wipe away my tears.

Every word of yours
Anchors me deeply.
I sink further,
Translucence transcending into opacity.

Boardwalk by the Beach

Let's skip across the planks,
Fingers interlaced indefinitely.
Hope our toes don't nick
The stray nail haphazardly hammered on.

Let's run through the scattered leaves.
A dance our steps will weave. Hope they don't
Worsen the cracks in the wood
Dampened by the crashing waves.

Let's pick the dandelions
That somehow sneaked through the gaps.
We'll blow them to each other's faces,
And succumb to sneezing fits at alternate
phases.

Let's go to the ice cream van
Selling perpetually overpriced sundaes.
We'll get two wooden spoons
And a banana split to share.

Let's lie on the seashore
Absorb the sun's radiating essence through our
core.
Dig out the discarded shards of seashells from
the sand,
And decorate our sandcastle.

Pray that the rising tides
Leave it unscathed.

Mirrors

You and I, one and the same.
Birthed from the same monster,
Left on the same shores as prey.
I chose to swim away.
You chose to remain.
Which one of us was braver?
Does it even matter,
When we're looking at each other now,
Face to face?
You roll your eyes at me mindlessly.
You think I had it all easy, being away from the
mess.
If that was the case,
Why am I next to you
On a rotting, drifting raft
Heading to who knows where?
All I know at this moment,
You being next to me,
Instils within me an indescribable sense so rare,
Of comfort and contentment, beyond compare.
Stay with me for a while.
As fleeting as it may be,
Let me indulge in the pleasure
Your unfailing presence brings me.

Wishful Thinking

My heart aches with the passing ticks
Of the clock hanging in the middle of my living
room.
I long for it to strike a chord within us both
And announce that it's finally time.

I wish we were in alignment.
Like the hours and minutes that synchronise
seamlessly,

Their hands intertwine regularly.
But we circle over and over endlessly
Like celestial bodies in orbit, gradually pulling
further away.

I pray for the cycles to end, to leave
This perpetual loop, to make the first move
To leave this sea of loneliness and step forward
Despite the lightyears it may take to reach you.

Infinitely stuck in the black hole of hesitation,
Hearts captured in a glitching simulation,
Thumbs break at the thought of communication.
Fears obscuring the pouring words.
Crashing into a glass wall like unwitting birds.

Bonfire

Flames flicker,
Minds wander.

My world was turned upside down
The moment our love was sown.

Words don't read like they're shown.

Tears that I stacked stone by stone
Flow down like molten gold.

Words don't speak like they're spoken.

Days of silence left me broken,
Hopes I built were brutally taken.

Words don't resonate anymore.

Loving you feels like a chore,
Wishing for the days before.

It Burns!

Salt from the sea breeze,
Tenderly stinging my eyes,
Blurring my vision.

Fish Bait

Here, fishy fishy!
Come and take the bait, don't fear.
Promise I won't bite,
Won't you hasten your gait, come near!

My time's ticking precisely,
My attention won't last long.
Affirm your affection firmly,
And my love will stand strong.

Swim out of the water,
See how long you'll last.
Look into my eyes,
And forget everything about your past.

Going back home?
Don't you think of such a thing!
Stay eternally by my side,
And revel in the pleasures I'll bring.

Seaward

The horizon blurs like watercolours
As the sun descends into the sea.
Hues of orange and blue
Dance the tango in melodic harmony.

The visible border tethering the two
Slowly fades out of my peripheral view.
The darkening sky poisons the water's
composition
The once pristine depths now infused with
shades of grey.

Like steamed milk being tainted with an
espresso shot
The moonlight provides a mild glow,
To the glaring blackness of the surroundings,
Illuminating the secret movements of the
seemingly still waters.

Raindrops gently perforate the surface,
Rippling the sea's smooth gaze.
Flowing waves attempt to escape the grasp of
their mother,
Rolling determinedly to uncertain shores.

Their desires prove unsuccessful
As repeated efforts result in their recession,
Rudely repelled seaward.

Heaven

Resting indoors, shoulder to shoulder.
Bodies aligned with the setting sun.
Your cheeks glow with soft amber hues.

I press my palms against them.
Your cheeks radiate with warmth,
As you burst into angelic laughter.

Your teeth shine like polished glass.
A beacon of hope within my dim light.
Guiding me through the maze of tangled nerves.

With you, my intrusive thoughts recede.
Within your gaze, I discover a tranquil
sanctuary,
Where I can quench my thirst, my reservations
freed.

Mental Block

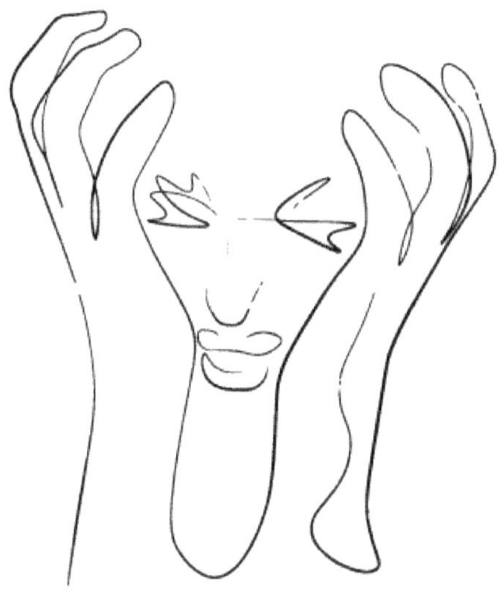

Inhibitions locked.
Creativity held at
Gunpoint, by my mind.

Stormy Day in the Neighbourhood

Shoulders stiff and tensed into place,
Bracing for the brutal impact
Of hail as heavy as bricks,
Crashing down onto my fraying umbrella.

The rain falls endlessly, a relentless cascade.
The city dilutes to a muted grey.
Puddles pooled within potholes overflow,
Transforming the streets into shallow rivers.

Separate bodies of water convene,
Forming an aquatic abomination like no other.
Secrets remain hidden under its surface,
The ripples emit them as whimsical whispers.

The frogs croak with boundless joy,
As their families gather for a summer pool party.
Their songs reverberate through the streets,
A euphony filling hearts with glee.

The stray neighbourhood cat squeals in fear,
Her polished coat was now a drenched mess.
She runs berserk, searching desperately for
shelter,

Hopes dampened by the rain's pelter.

I crouch down and scoop her into my arms,
Her shivering body, too exhausted to resist.
She snuggles peacefully into my elbow,
Finding solace, her fears gradually mellow.

Bliss beyond belief,
In this temporary moment of strife.
As we stand together in the middle of the street,
Being confined to the rain's harsh embrace.

Hypervigilant

Sensations amplify tenfold
When you walk into my room.

The air thickens quickly like syrup
Sickly sweet, it creeps into every crevice
Dense and heavy, I sink to the ground like a
block of cement.

My feet fuse with the floor tiles.
Frozen in position, they turn to marble
The sculpture to your creator
Each fleeting look you give carves deeply
I'm a fawn caught in your hypnotising
headlights

My pupils dilate, expanding my peripheral
vision.
I follow every minute movement of yours,
Beads of sweat pool on my lip.
My desires entangle with unending fears
My brain mocks my prudishness, yet categorises
desire as a vice

I hang precariously on the precipice I built
As I teeter on the edge of this red abyss,
I take a leap of faith, plunging into the depths of
your soul,
As explosive as fireworks, a mirror to my hidden
self.

Will the ignition of my passion,
Fuel our budding love like gasoline?
Or will it be futile, reducing me to smouldering
embers?

Withering

Years of relentless fighting, a futile campaign.
My arduous efforts, ending in vain.
Reduced into grovelling the sand like a starving
puppy,

Digging furiously for remains.

Spread thin like butter on a burnt base,
My malleable essence was stretched until it was
taut.
Frays began to form, clumping together like
dead knots.
They curved away from my body in twisted
fronds.

Spores, painstakingly grown, took flight with the
wind.
My physical vessel left floating aimlessly and
hollow.
I glued the rotting twigs over my palms in a
crosshatch design,
A desperate attempt to deflect the shame that
follows.

The Pigeon Whisperer

A lone presence among the bustle of the city,
She gazes solemnly, intently registering,
The chaotic scene unfolding before her.

An electric clash between two pigeons,
Duelling to a certain death.
Miniature as they seem,
They behave as beasts, malice evident in their
eyes' gleams.

Their iridescent plumage, tinged violet with rage
and green with envy,
Beaks curved in a menacing smile; wings raised
with fury.
Their chests puffed with a prideful air, they
crash into each other.

The Whisperer sighs in exasperation, lips
crinkled in wry amusement.
Easing herself from the bench, she arms her fists
with breadcrumbs.
Perfecting her aim, she shoots them like
missiles,
The particles falling upon the birds, deafeningly
like drums.

With the mischievous pigeons stunned into
stillness,
She springs to swift action.
With seasoned precision, she pried them apart.
Pointing their beaks to their meal on the grass,
She announces the feast's start.

Jellyfish

Bioluminescent.
You billow with blue.

Your translucent skin
Reflecting beauty so bright,
Blinding everything unpleasant with your
essence,
Erasing shadows of doubt, leaving behind
Peace and purity.

Glittering tassels,
Flowing like lace,
Glowing like dew drops,
Mesmerising every creature
In your flowery path lit by fairy lights.

You never let me in fully.
You keep yourself in hiding.
Fearing your sting
Will keep me away.

Sweet butterfly of mine,
For you, I will
Plunge into the depths of the sea,
Protect you from every danger,

Purge every lingering fear.

Trust in me,
My love for you goes deep.

Escapism

With a dream's embrace,
Reality is concealed
Easing my burdens

A Cafe Rendezvous

Amongst the chaos in the city,
We find a quaint cafe, adorned with green.
A slice of flora, served on a banana leaf.

The deafening streets fade far behind,
Your presence muffles the permeating noise.
We unwind seamlessly in the silence.

Bursts of sunlight shine vibrantly through the
semi-open blinds
You raise your hand, shielding my eyes.
Unmoving until the clouds move to block the
sun.

We order tiramisu, the caffeine's embrace
Sustaining us through the day
Reluctant to part, we stroll aimlessly, basking in
romance.

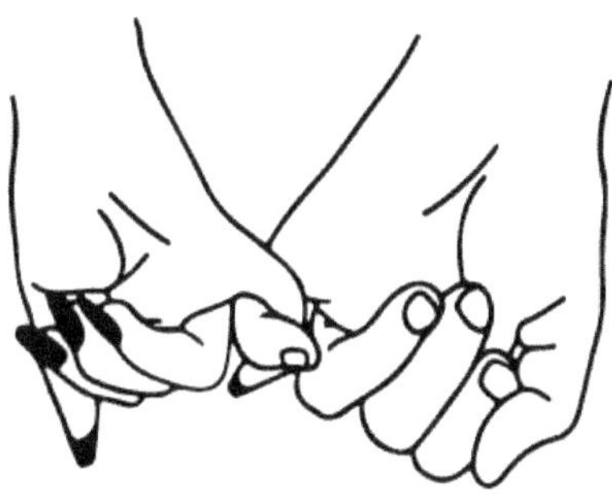